APR   2007

WALKINGSTICKS

by Patrick Merrick

The Child's World

Content Adviser:
Jeffrey Hahn,
Department of Entomology,
University of Minnesota

Published in the United States of America by The Child's World®
PO Box 326 • Chanhassen, MN 55317-0326
800-599-READ • www.childsworld.com

PHOTO CREDITS
© AP Photo/John D. McHugh: 12
© David A. Northcott/Corbis: 7
© Dr. William J. Weber/Visuals Unlimited: 20–21
© Fletcher & Baylis/Photo Researchers, Inc.: 13
© John T. Fowler/Alamy: 5
© Kevin Schafer/Alamy: 15
© Lawrence Lawry/Photo Researchers, Inc.: 29
© Mary Clay/Dembinsky Photo Associates: 11
© Maximilian Weinzierl/Alamy: 24, 27
© Piotr Naskrecki/Minden Pictures: 18
© Robert & Linda Mitchell: cover, 1, 6, 9, 16, 19, 23

ACKNOWLEDGMENTS
The Child's World®: Mary Berendes, Publishing Director;
Katherine Stevenson, Editor

The Design Lab: Kathleen Petelinsek, Design and Page Production

LIBRARY OF CONGRESS CATALOGING-IN-PUBLICATION DATA
Merrick, Patrick.
 Walkingsticks / by Patrick Merrick.
  p. cm. — (New naturebooks)
 Includes bibliographical references and index.
 ISBN 1-59296-654-3 (library bound : alk. paper)
 1. Stick insects—Juvenile literature. I. Title. II. Series.
 QL509.5.M48 2006
 595.7'29—dc22   2006001381

Table of Contents

On the cover: An orange-winged walkingstick moves slowly across a leaf in Malaysia.

Meet the Walkingstick!

Walkingsticks have been around for at least 150 million years.

It's a warm afternoon, and a bird is flitting through the forest, looking for a late lunch. The bird lands on a branch and studies the twigs and leaves around it, hoping to find a tasty bug. No luck! The bird hops along the branch, then gives up and flies away. Hours later, the sun has set, and darkness settles over the forest. Suddenly, one of the twigs where the bird was sitting starts to move—and then gets up and walks away! A close look shows that this "twig" isn't really a twig at all. What is it? It's a walkingstick!

Northern walkingsticks like this one are very common in the United States and parts of southern Canada. They grow to be about 3 inches (8 cm) long and look a lot like twigs.

What Are Walkingsticks?

"Phasmatodea" comes from the Latin word *phasma*, which means "phantom." The name refers to the way the insects match their surroundings so closely that they seem to disappear.

Walkingsticks belong to a group of **insects** called Phasmatodea. The insects in this group tend to look amazingly like the plants on which they live. The Phasmatodea group includes both stick insects, which look like twigs, and leaf insects, which look like plant leaves.

Like other insects, walkingsticks have three main body parts—a head, a midsection (**thorax**), and a tail section (**abdomen**). They also have three pairs of legs. Most insects have one or two pairs of wings, but most walkingsticks have wings too small for flying, or no wings at all.

This page shows the bright wings of an orange-winged walkingstick. On the facing page you can see the twiglike body of a New Guinea spiny stick.

What Do Walkingsticks Look Like?

Walkingsticks range in color from the bright green of plant leaves to the gray and brown of sticks. Some are a solid color, while others have patterns.

Walkingsticks have both claws and sucker-like pads on their feet to help them move about on different types of surfaces.

Walkingsticks are strange—they look so much like plants, it's hard to believe they're insects! Their shape and coloring act as **camouflage**, making the insects very hard to see and protecting them from animals that would try to eat them.

Many kinds of walkingsticks have long, thin bodies and legs that make them look like twigs or grass. Even their feelers, or **antennae**, are long. Some walkingsticks have more rounded or flattened bodies that look like other plant parts, such as leaves. Some have lumps, bumps, spikes, or other unusual shapes that match those of certain plants. Even their legs are sometimes shaped like plant parts.

This giant Malaysian walkingstick's camouflage helps it blend in with the tree on which it lives. The insect holds its antennae straight out in front of itself to look more like a twig.

Where Do Walkingsticks Live?

Young Australian walkingsticks use a great trick to stay safe—they look and act like scorpions. Thinking the insects are the real thing, most enemies stay away!

There are about 2,000 different kinds, or **species**, of walkingsticks. Walkingsticks are found in many areas of the world, although most of them live in warmer regions. North America has about 40 species. Elsewhere, they live in southern Europe, Asia, Africa, Australia, and Central and South America.

Walkingsticks look different depending on where they live. The kinds that live in North America look like small twigs and branches. Those that live in jungles tend to be bigger, and many have sharp spines that look like thorns. In China and the Far East, walkingsticks have flatter legs and bodies that look like the flat leaves of the trees that grow in those regions.

Australian walkingsticks like this one live in New Guinea and northern Australia. They grow to be about 5 inches (13 cm) long and are covered with spines and bumps to blend in with their rainforest surroundings.

How Big Are Walkingsticks?

Some larger kinds of walkingsticks have big spines on their legs.

Walkingsticks range in size from very short to very long. The most common walkingstick in North America, the northern walkingstick, grows between three and four inches (8 and 10 cm) long. The smallest walkingsticks in North America are only about one-half inch (12 mm) in length, and the longest grow to about 7 inches (18 cm).

Other areas of the world are home to much larger walkingsticks. In fact, the longest insect ever recorded was a giant walkingstick from West Malaysia that measured nearly 22 inches (over 55 cm)! Other species grow to about half that size.

Here you can see two sizes of the giant Malaysian walkingstick. This page shows a newly hatched baby. The facing page shows an adult crawling on a woman's shirt.

What Do Walkingsticks Eat?

Some kinds of walkingsticks eat grasses.

Since walkingsticks don't fly, they must walk from one tree to another. Sometimes trees on one side of a road or stream will be completely stripped of leaves, while those on the other side suffer little damage.

Walkingsticks eat the leaves of trees, shrubs, and other types of plants. In North America, northern walkingsticks especially like the leaves of oak, black cherry, black locust, and sassafrass trees, as well as clover. Most of the time, walkingsticks' leaf-eating is not a problem. Occasionally, if there are too many walkingsticks, they can eat all the leaves off an entire stand of trees!

Some people keep walkingsticks as pets, since these insects don't bite or sting and they're so interesting to look at. People usually feed pet walkingsticks leaves from plants such as brambles (blackberries), raspberries, strawberries, roses, ivy, and oak.

14

This hungry walkingstick is eating a leaf in Colombia's La Planada Nature Reserve.

How Do Walkingsticks Stay Safe?

Sometimes walkingsticks shake their bodies or sway gently with the breeze, to blend in with nearby leaves and branches that are also moving.

Walkingsticks often hold their front legs straight out, alongside their antennae. That makes them look even more like twigs.

Many animals, such as lizards, birds, and spiders, will eat walkingsticks if they get the chance. **Parasitic** wasps and flies also try to lay their eggs on walkingstick eggs, so that the young wasps or flies can feed on the young walkingsticks. But walkingsticks have some interesting ways of protecting themselves from their **predators**.

First, they blend in with their surroundings so well that they are really hard to find. Even their eggs look like plant seeds. Walkingsticks are also active at night, or **nocturnal**. During the day, they keep perfectly still for hours, so predators can't see them. At night, they move around and feed, but they don't usually move very far.

Giant walkingsticks live in the southern U.S. and are the longest insects in North America, growing to 7 inches (18 cm). There are six giant walkingsticks in this picture, taken in Texas. Can you find them all?

Goliath walkingsticks like this one have another trick for staying safe—their tail end looks like a snake that's about to strike! Goliath walkingsticks live in Australia.

Besides their camouflage, walkingsticks have other tricks to help them escape from predators. If a walkingstick is grabbed, disturbed, or pecked, it often goes stiff and plays dead. That can mean tucking up its legs and falling all the way from a high tree branch to the ground. The walkingstick stays completely still until the predator leaves. Once the danger is gone, the walkingstick gets up and slowly climbs the tree again.

Some walkingsticks curl their abdomens up over their backs, making them look like poisonous scorpions, which have stingers on the ends of their tails.

This Costa Rican walkingstick is showing its eyespot. When threatened, this walkingstick opens its wings to reveal the "eye." This makes the insect look much bigger and scarier than it really is. Thinking the walkingstick is more trouble than it's worth, most attackers will leave it alone.

19

Many walkingsticks also have body parts that put out bad-tasting, bad-smelling, or harmful liquids. Some types have nasty-tasting liquids that they spit up or that ooze from their legs. Others spray a liquid out of their thorax that causes pain and temporary blindness in attackers—even in people!

Walkingsticks have another kind of protection that is really unusual. When something grabs some walkingsticks, especially young ones, the walkingstick simply loses a leg—and then grows it back! Walkingsticks are the only insects that can grow back body parts.

A young walkingstick can grow a new leg in only a couple of weeks.

Two-striped walkingsticks like this one are also called "musk mares." This name refers to their ability to squirt a smelly liquid (sometimes called musk) *from their thorax. These walkingsticks are common in Florida.*

21

How Are Baby Walkingsticks Born?

Male walking-sticks are rare. For some walkingstick species, no males have ever been found! Instead, the females lay eggs that turn into exact copies of the mother.

Female walkingsticks lay eggs that are hard and shiny and look like small seeds. Sometimes, the eggs look exactly like the seeds of the plants on which the insects live.

Some walkingstick species bury their eggs in the ground, lay them in holes in plants or in loose leaves on the ground, or glue them to leaves or tree bark. In some cases, the eggs hatch in the same season. In other cases, the eggs sit for months or over a year before hatching.

Here you can see some giant Malaysian walkingstick eggs. They all fell on the same leaf on the forest floor.

Many types of walkingsticks lay their eggs high up in trees, and the eggs then drop all the way to the ground. That can be a long way! If lots of female walkingsticks live in one tree, it looks and sounds as if it is raining eggs.

These kinds of eggs have a part that contains fats and other substances ants like to eat. Some types of ants carry the eggs back to their nests, bite off the part they want to use for food, then throw the rest away with the garbage. The walkingstick eggs lie with the other old garbage, safe from all sorts of dangers. Months later, the eggs hatch—often, right inside the ant nest.

Sometimes huge numbers of walkingstick eggs end up on the ground. Under some North American trees, people have counted over a hundred eggs on every square foot (almost one square meter) of ground.

In colder areas, adult walkingsticks die when the first frosts of winter come.

Here you can see a young Vietnamese walkingstick as it hatches out of its egg. These walkingsticks live in Vietnam and Southeast Asia.

25

What Are Baby Walkingsticks Like?

After molting, a young walkingstick eats its old, dried-up skin.

Young walkingsticks can take three months to a year to become adults.

When walkingstick eggs hatch, the babies look like little adults. They are active and take care of themselves right from the start, climbing up nearby plants to feed on them. They start on lower plants and climb higher as they grow.

Young walkingsticks spend several months growing. Because of their hard, shell-like skin, they can't grow steadily, the way people do. Instead, when they get too big for their hard skin, they shed it, or **molt**. A new, bigger skin is waiting underneath. A walkingstick molts up to seven times before it becomes an adult.

This picture shows an adult Vietnamese walkingstick with several younger ones. Vietnamese walkingsticks grow to be about 5 inches (13 cm) long. They are often found on blackberry bushes.

Can We Learn More about Walkingsticks?

Depending on the species, walkingsticks can live for just a few months or up to two years.

In Malaysia, people keep jungle nymph walkingsticks and feed them guava leaves, then make tea from their droppings.

Scientists still have lots to learn about these ancient life forms! In fact, there are types of walkingsticks that have never even been named or described. People studying rain forests and other places with lots of insect life will keep finding new information on stick insects.

Walkingsticks are some of the most interesting insects in the world. People love to look at them—if they can find them! Sometimes, though, it's hard to see walkingsticks even when they're right in front of your nose. If you watch very carefully, you might be lucky enough to see one in the wild!

Jungle nymph walkingsticks like this one are very common in Malaysia. They have thorns all over their bodies, which helps them blend in with the thorny bushes where they live. Jungle nymphs can be up to 6 inches (15 cm) long.

Glossary

abdomen (AB-duh-mun) On insects and some other animals, the abdomen is the entire rear section of the body. Walkingsticks have a very long abdomen.

antennae (an-TEH-nee) Antennae are movable feelers on the heads of insects and some other animals that help them find out about their surroundings. Walkingsticks have very long antennae.

camouflage (KA-muh-flazh) Camouflage is special coloring or markings that help an animal blend in with its surroundings. Walkingsticks' camouflage makes them look like branches and leaves.

insects (IN-sekts) Insects are boneless animals that have six legs, three main body parts (a head, a thorax, and an abdomen), and usually one or two pairs of wings.

molt (MOLT) To molt is to get rid of an old outer layer of skin, shell, hair, or feathers. Walkingsticks molt up to seven times before becoming adults.

nocturnal (nok-TUR-nul) An animal that is nocturnal is active mostly at night and rests during the day. Walkingsticks are nocturnal.

parasitic (payr-uh-SIH-tik) Parasitic plants or animals live on or inside other living things, feeding off of them. Some parasitic wasps and flies live on young walkingsticks.

predators (PREH-duh-terz) Predators are animals that hunt and kill other animals for food. Some predators eat walkingsticks.

species (SPEE-sheez) An animal species is a group of animals that share the same features and can have babies only with animals in the same group. There are about 2,000 different species of walkingsticks.

thorax (THOR-aks) An insect's thorax is the middle section of its body. Walkingsticks usually have a long thorax.

To Find Out More

Read It!

Green, Tamara, and Tony Gibbons (illustrator). *Walking Sticks*. Milwaukee, WI: Gareth Stevens, 1997.

Harris, Monica. *Walking Stick*. Chicago, IL: Heinemann Library, 2003.

Kelly, Diane A. *Stick Insect*. Detroit, MI: Kidhaven Press, 2005.

Watts, Barrie. *Stick Insects*. New York: Franklin Watts, 1991.

On the Web

Visit our home page for lots of links about walkingsticks: *http://www.childsworld.com/links*

Note to Parents, Teachers, and Librarians: We routinely check our Web links to make sure they're safe, active sites—so encourage your readers to check them out!

31

Index

About the Author

When Pat Merrick was a child, his family traveled and moved many times. He became fascinated with science and finding out about the world around him. In college he majored in science and education. After college, Mr. Merrick and his wife both decided to become teachers and try and help kids learn to love the world around them. He has taught science to all levels of kids, from kindergarten through twelfth grade. When not teaching or writing, Mr. Merrick loves to read and play with his six children. He currently lives in a small town in southern Minnesota with his wife and family.